AF265091

Poems for You

SPIRITUAL AND INSPIRATIONAL THEMES

Kay Meade

Copyright © 2020 Kay Meade
Second edition

Earth Message Press
www.earthmessagepress.com/contact-us

ISBN 978-0-473-29183-9

All rights reserved. No part of this publication may be copied, reproduced or transmitted in any form or by any means without the permission of the publishers.

Compiled by *Peter Ashley*
Cover illustration *Peter Ashley*
Copy editing and design *Peter Ashley*

Humanity hold the greatest value commodity
– love –
and yet it is undiscovered in many
and not valued by others.

Love is the Key – so always let it be!

Contents

Introduction

I have channelled messages and been guided to write what you are about to read. Spiritual guidance is given in many different ways, and verses that rhyme is one of these ways.

We are all touched by or drawn to different things. If verse is your way, I hope that you are touched by these.

Your new day

Today is new and awaits you
Yesterday no longer can be entered into
Forward you go into a new day.

With Love your daily foundation
Dreams and achievements enter creation
People you meet amplify determination,
To integrate love into realization.

When you and you and you…
Transmit love's pure vibration
Hope is given to all global nations
A future certain for this and future generations.

Embraced in love's elation
All that there is, is in harmonization
Confidently you go into each new day.

Morning glory

I looked above the cherry trees and saw a cloak of morning cloud

Little by little, the cloak parted to glowing edged frothy clouds

Revealing the secreted beauty of the blue sky and the golden sun.

Light shone in now and everything about me looked enriched

As it reflected the beauty of what was above.

New day dawning

Please remember

Each new day dawning

Is an opening in time for exploring

To discover your calling

And know that love is your mooring

Your four letter word LOVE will stop the warring

Of the thoughts you are thinking

Of the words you are saying

And all of your acts of doing

And will be balance restoring.

Pure gold

Love is the story to be told
The reason being it is pure gold
This story needs to continue to be sold
Until all live in Love's mould
Then your world will be the Light to behold
As glory will reign as foretold.
Love is the assuring of life enduring.

Declare your love

Humankind,

Declare your love for the All That There Is

Not just once but each and everyday you live.

Your love declaration becomes your avowed intention

To change the overall frequency of Humankind's vibration.

The vibrations of individual humans are wavering and waning,

Oscillating and draining the combined level of Humankind's vibration.

Move away from hate.

Move away from your material and self-interest obsessions.

Discover your connection to the love vibration of the

All That There Is, and once you have found it, commit to it.

Commit to, and live by, this profound Love.

This will bring about balance and development to

The combined frequency of Humankind's vibration.

Stand united for love alone, and bring light to the Earth plane.

Affect the change that the Love vibrations at play make possible

And your birth right will be yours once more.

The real world plan

Love is the real world plan - all else is an illusion

Love will not make you live in fear

Love will not take away your freedom

Be guided by and express the love that you are

Be part of the real world plan.

I am the spirit within

When you look in a mirror
The reflection you see is not really me
It is merely the human form you see
I am the spirit within, the essence of thee
Please find and treasure me.

When you find me
I can help you be all that you can be
I am love, I am perfect and whole
For I am divine you see
And that is how you too can be
When you find and treasure me.

I have been with you for all time
And when you acknowledge me
You will know your purpose and at one be
United we'll shine and reflect the source divine
So when you look in the mirror of life
You will see me.

Home is near

Be peaceful, and

Let the embodiment of you know HOME is near

Sense cobweb touches so gentle and dear

Hear whispering voices become so clear

Accept willingly energy vibrations to touch your core

And let the power of your spirit be assured to steer.

Love and peace

At the centre of all people of the earthly plane
There is always great love and peace.
The discovery of this love and peace,
And the use of this love and peace
Is humanity's power to create the earthly
Plane envisioned for humankind.

The angels call

The angels are calling me early this morning
It is just after four
And nowhere near my time of dawning
Yet to me the angels seem to be calling.

As I arise I hear them say...
There are multiplicious options available each day
Stay focused, deviate not, don't let the past
Or others, lead you astray
Keep transitioning, from what you are not
To what you are, each and every day.

Accumulate and nurture the riches of love
And only this display
For all else is illusionary
And not relevant to the game of life in play
Love is the constant and yet the evolving essence
Of the human state
Please remember this - everyday.

Part of All

Every soul that embodied be
Is not without
But is still with me.

Remember

Remember to remember
That you are a member
Of the life-stream of the Creator.

You hold the power of love.

When you re-member
You will be that love.

Morning

In the morning
Choose your dawning
And deliver unyielding
Your essence revealing
Your love – and be truly appealing.

In love – when you are truly appealing
You will attract all right dealings
And bring unto yourself all needed feelings
Ensuring all healings
To expand your love and be more truly appealing.

When love is expanding
It is really rewarding
Not only for you, but those quietly urging
"Be from the heart, be your calling"
Because then, you will be most truly appealing.

The key

Turn the key
And discover me
The Light within thee.

Then you will see
What you will truly be.

Crystallise your reality

Do you have clarity of your reality?
Your reality crystallises the nearer you
get to your spirituality
As then you know there is no duality
Oneness is all that there is in reality.

Love, happiness and peace

Where there is love, there is happiness
Where there is happiness, there is love.

And where there is love, there is peace
Where there is peace, there is hope.

Hope for a future of love, happiness and peace.

A loving heart

A loving heart is full of forgiveness
Opening the eyes to see with compassion
And the mind to be understanding
And have reverence for life.

So always be your loving heart.

When

When eyes see beauty

And ears hear laughter

When the senses are awakened to the day's fresh fragrances

When mouths speak only kind and guiding words

When arms embrace

When hands help

When fingers no longer point

When legs march only for peace

When feet dance in joy

When minds unite to create good

And there is respect for all

Then the heart and soul will sing with love.

Enjoy the beauty of creation

Welcome the energy of the elements each day

Receive refreshment from the cleansing rain

And strength from the force of the wind

Let the sun energise and warm you

And let a blanketing of snow

Provide fun for the child within

There is beauty and wonderment in all of creation

Absorb it and reflect it.

Angels of the Light

The Angels of the Light
Give to you a star, so bright
To illuminate your darkest night
And watch over your special life.

The Angels of the Light
Send you healing beams of Light
To ensure you're fit and right
So you will soar to great heights.

The Angels of the Light
Walk with you day and night
To enhance your life with Love and Light
So you will know you are Light.

The Angels of the Light
Proclaim in melodies of delight
You are a being of divine Light
And are free to BE by divine right.

Let me guide you

Dance with me in the moonlight tonight
Feel my embrace, so gentle yet tight
Let me guide you in this dance – called life
And move in rhythm, as one, tonight.

Dance with me in the moonlight tonight
Feel joy and happiness for life ignite
Let this flame for life spread much Light
As we move in rhythm, as one, tonight.

Dance with me in the moonlight tonight
Feel adventure and courage for life alight
Let your lodestar guide you aright
As we move in rhythm, as one, tonight.

Dance with me in the moonlight tonight
Feel wisdom and knowledge infuse your might
Let this flow in all your dealings in life
As we move in rhythm, as one, tonight.

Dance with me in the moonlight tonight

Feel my love and know you're just right

Let this be your power to abundance in life

As we move in rhythm, as one, tonight.

Healers unite with the Light

Healers unite tonight
Be channels for the Light
To deliver much needed sight
To the seekers of the Light.

Unite with the Light tonight
The seekers of the Light
Be awakened to your might
So you can always live in Light.

Awakened to the Light
You gain special sight
To see the true delights
At one with the Light, all is right.

Time to shine

It is time for you to shine
To attract those who seek to align
To the energy so pure and fine
That unites the spirit with the divine.

Fusion with the divine
Will nurture the spirit for all time
Empowering with love sublime
Another prism of the Light to shine.

Each prism of Light magnifies and defines
The purpose of heaven on Earth to outshine
For life is love and love is life divine
So those aligned will always, always shine.

Be yourself today

Let the provenance of your being BE today

Let only the energy of Source within you BE today

This is the natural essence of each and everyone upon the Earth plane.

So be yourself today and every day

And let your provenance be what on Earth does reign.

Purest form of existence

In the energy of love is the purest form of existence

It is the consciousness of All That There Is

It is for all

It is like the stars in your heavens

It is always there.

All ways

Always, and in all ways

I am with you

You are born of My Light

I am you, as you are Me

I am Love, so you are Love

I am with you already

And always will be

Accept, allow, and greet My Love

Alight the loving Light of graciousness

Then, as one presence on Earth, exist.

The new you!

A new day

A new month

A new year

A new you ...

When you

Listen to hear me

Look to see me

Think to find me

Live to be as me, then ...

You will be Love

You will be Me

Love needs to be!

Emerge ...

The new you!

The Creator's breeze

The trees stir in graceful movement from the Creator's breeze

Awakening sounds of nature to float in the air with ease

Gentle is the voice that calls for you to hear and heed

So listen, for the sounds that float in the air with ease.

The trees stir in graceful movement from the Creator's breeze

Manifesting visions of unity to be seen with ease

Beautiful is the sight shown for you to see and heed

So watch for visions of unity that can be seen with ease.

The trees stir in graceful movement from the Creator's breeze

Yielding an abundant bounty to be enjoyed with ease

Luscious is this nourishment for you to have and heed

So take nurture from the bounty that can be had with ease.

The trees stir in graceful movement from the Creator's breeze

Showing that when harmony exists, there is ease

Empowering your being with all that you need

Your tree of life stirs, empowered, ready to reign and please.

Signs

As you walk your path you will see many signs
Signs that will help you, and guide you on your way.

Do not be blind to these signs
They can be but a beautiful flower
That greets you on a dull day
Or it can be the wondrous moon
That gleams down shining its light on you.

Signs are all about you
And we offer them readily when you ask
"What is on your path and where are you to go?"

These signs are there – just look a little further
Let your eyes open wide
Let us help you on your way.

The 2012 year

The 2012 year is here

So let the beauty of your time appear

Let the Light so rare

And love so dear

Be manifest in you and all those for whom you care.

So ask through prayer

That you discover this year

That what you are is clear

So Light and love on Earth appear

In this much awaited year.

United in love will steer

Proclamation of the gifts you bear

And the golden rain will be here

So the great magnificence will appear

Connecting you to the one who cares.

This poem was written in 2012 but is relevant to every age and time.

New morning

Feel the calmness of the new morning
Greet you with much love and hope.

Feel the new energy greet your beingness this morning
As the awakening of the purpose of the soul is manifested.

11-11-11 verse

We hear you ask, what is happening today?

Well the universe aligns this day
To the energies from far away
Ensuring Earth a passageway
Within the White Light Ray.

Celebrate this wonderful day
Earth now rides the love energy sway
And the universe welcomes it to stay
Within the White Light Ray.

All elements unite this day
Earth, humankind and the heavens say
Earth comes of age this day
At one with the White Light Ray.

I was guided to write this poem on 11.11.2011.

The energy rises

The soul, the essence of thee
Is purpose aware and ready to steer
For Earth and humanity to ascend their sphere
And bring in the time for the great magnificence to appear
And so, the energy rises.

The soul, the essence of thee
Releases love for heaven and Earth to see
Love shining brightly bridges these stratospheres
Connected by love the ascension way is crystal clear
And so, the energy rises.

The soul, the essence of thee
Embraced now by heaven's love and Earth's zeal
Manifests a golden shield that protects and heals
Earth and humanity enter their new age as love revealed
And so, the energy rises, and the great magnificence is sealed.

Love is the Key, so always let it be.

The gift

Upon the Earth he came and walked

He played, he learnt, and then about love he taught

He revered his Father and his given task in faith sought

He gave of himself so love would be in all who on the Earth walked

So special is the gift he gave, when accepted will welcome in a new age

Accept, accept and bring to be the love in thee and all that be.

In my Father's name

Unto the Earth I came
And worked in my Father's name
For great was his pain
That love on Earth did not reign.

I left through pain
Knowing that love on Earth could reign
And my Father's pain could wane
As humankind would evolve and change.

Humankind – stop making the pain!
You each hold the key of love for change
Turn the key and let love be on your plane
And see my Father's Divine Plan on Earth reign.

In the hour of my greatest pain
Love was my sustain
You will surely gain
When you trust in my Father's name.

You are all of the same

It is not in my Father's name
That in parts of the earthly plane
Humankind are acting out such destructive 'games'
Inflicting pain, oh such pain and hurt that kills and maims
To their own kind – but ones they see as not the same
And all for what but selfish, senseless gain.

You need to know that you are all of the same
Yet unique to shine your special flame
So live the love of understanding game
With ALL, compassionately cooperate and explain
As that is how humankind on Earth will gain
Then and only then will it be in my Father's name.

Christmas message

Christmas is about to be celebrated this year
With family and friends that you hold dear
But is the purpose of this celebration clear
Or is it seen only as a way to gain more gear?

Foster the meaning true this Christmas time of year
The remembrance of the baby Jesus dear
The gift of love given for all to know and share
So that humanity would no longer need to fear.

You see Christmas is a 'Giving' time of year
And a time for all to be full of joy and cheer
For the love and hope given that first Christmas time year
So celebrate this gift so unique and rare.

Spare no cost this Christmas time of year
Give the most precious, priceless gifts you have to share
The gifts of Love and Hope to those you hold dear
For these are real treasures to be enjoyed in every year.

Parable of the birds

I sit and watch the birds at play
From behind my tinted window pane
And from my vantage point I see
But they don't see me.

The birds they sing and hop and play
They squabble and jostle on the feeding tray
They eat for themselves and for others they take away
And when all in the tray is gone they fly away.

The birds still sing and hop and play
But are no longer seen from my window pane.

Above the cherry trees

Above the cherry trees a grey cloak
Of morning cloud, blankets the sky
Little by little the cloak parts
To glowing edged frothy clouds
Revealing the secreted beauty
Of the blue sky and the golden sun
Immediately Light shines through
The cherry trees, stirring everything
To mirror and shine forth
The beauty of what is always above
Part your personal clouds
And reflect your sparkling light!
See the verve of your being
Transformed, and your world
Illuminated by The Light

Cooperation

From my tinted window pane I see

The birds fly into the olive tree

It seems with pleasure they chirp and sing

Wings flutter and branches spring

As they seek their breakfast on the wing

And as they feast they preen the olive tree.

It seems the birds and the olive tree are showing me

That work needs to be enjoyed

And where cooperation exists much will be gained.

So I'm encouraged by the birds and the olive tree

And will set about my days with glee

Enjoying what is before me.

The sounds in the silence

It is so very quiet this early morn
It is long before the dawn
The pendulum movement of the clock on the wall
Is the only sound I hear.

Now the silence of the morn draws me
Into another space of time
My ears now hear with amazing clarity
The harmonious sounds of this silent space.

No longer I hear the call of the clock on the wall
The sounds in the silence are close by
And yet also seem from far away
Layers upon layers of sound talking to me
Guiding the part of me
That knows the sounds in the silence.

I feel so at peace in this space
I want to stay bathed by the sounds in the silence.
I didn't seem to be there very long
When the morn came
The birds sang and the clock called
I pulled open the curtains and saw a new day dawn.

Magpies

Magpies are curious birds
They spend their time gathering things that shine
They make these things their own
Without any thought from whence they came.

A magpie you should not be
For unique and special you each be
You have all that shines within thee
On your path, seek and gather giving credit where due
Then you will be the truth of you.

Announcing the new day

It is early morn

All is calm, crisp and clear

Only the birds seem to be at work and play

Their chirps fill the air

Excitedly announcing the new day.

Tapestry of life

Stitch every stitch of your tapestry of life
And allow it to reflect who you are
Everything in balance – everything just right
Fun, happiness, joy, experience, upsets
All are what make life
Let your stitching start
Every one with care, every one just right
Because you're with the Light.

Love on Earth

Accept the energies anew on your plane
They will guide you to evolve and change
And strengthen your resolve
To be an instrument to bring in change
And make love on Earth the known game.

Reap before you sleep

Before you sleep

We ask that you reap

The wisdom of our speak

Because we divulge what you seek.

Keep searching

It will help the Earth plane to let your essence reign
Do not let your search for what you are wane
Because this is the time to keep searching
Even if you feel you have reached knowledge.

Continue, continue to seek and expand
Expand the knowledge and learn about yourself
In doing that you will let your essence reign
And you will help the Earth gain.

There is only love
So find the love and let it reign.

Be all that you are
Seek only to be all that you are
Only all that you are
There is nothing else to be.

No limitations

Vast are you

Vast is your potential

You are the only one limiting you.

The Light

Light is all that is needed
Realise that the Light is within and without you
So love yourself and love all that is about you.

Feel the harmony – it radiates from the Light
The Light is peace, and the Light gives all that is needed
Reach out for the Light always
Embrace the Light and feel the harmony.

The soul needs the love, it needs the peace
And it needs the harmony that comes from the Light
Open yourselves to this Light.

You are the Light – remember you are always the Light
You are One, you are the Light
Feel the Oneness – be at one with the Light
Unite with the Light!

About the author

Kay Meade is a trance medium who has been channelling messages from the 'Circle of The Light of The Love Energy', a group of spiritual beings, since mid 2009.

Kay and husband Peter Ashley live in New Zealand.

For further information about the authors, their books and meditation CDs, and the latest messages from The Circle of The Light of The Love Energy go to www.earthmessage-press.com.

The authors welcome any feedback or questions related to this book at www.earthmessagepress.com/contact-us.

Other books by the author include:

Earth Messages of the Love Energy

Love is the Key

Lily and the Pink Pyramid (illustrated children's book published under the author's married name Kay Ashley)

www.ingramcontent.com/pod-product-compliance
Lightning Source LLC
Chambersburg PA
CBHW050000070726

47592CB00019B/1694